Koalas

Steve Parish

ANIMALS are Fun!

For a free color catalog describing Gareth Stevens Publishing's list of high-quality books and multimedia programs, call 1-800-542-2595 (USA) or 1-800-461-9120 (Canada). Gareth Stevens Publishing's Fax: (414) 225-0377.

Library of Congress Cataloging-in-Publication Data available upon request from the publisher. Fax: (414) 225-0377 for the attention of the Publishing Records Department.

ISBN 0-8368-2615-9

First published in North America in 2000 by
Gareth Stevens Publishing
1555 North RiverCenter Drive, Suite 201
Milwaukee, WI 53212 USA

This edition © 2000 by Gareth Stevens, Inc. First published in 1998 by Steve Parish Publishing Pty. Ltd., P. O. Box 1058, Archerfield, BC, Queensland 4108, Australia. Original edition © 1998 by Steve Parish Publishing Pty. Ltd. Photography and creative direction by Steve Parish. Text by E. Melanie Lever, Kate Lovett, and Pat Slater, SPP. Additional end matter © 2000 by Gareth Stevens, Inc.

U.S. author: Amy Bauman

Printed in the United States of America

1 2 3 4 5 6 7 8 9 04 03 02 01 00

Gareth Stevens Publishing
MILWAUKEE

The koala is a small, furry, warm-blooded mammal.

It is known as a marsupial.
The female has a pouch.

A koala has two thumbs on each of its front paws for gripping.

When a baby is born, it crawls into its mother's pouch.

The baby stays inside the pouch until it has fur and can see.

When it is older, a baby koala rides on its mother's back.

The koala's thick, woolly fur keeps it warm and dry.

This is important for an animal that lives outside in the trees.

A koala eats leaves from eucalyptus, or gum, trees.

It climbs from tree to tree
to find the right leaves.

Leaves do not give the koala much energy, so it sleeps a lot.

When the air is cold, a koala often curls up and takes a nap.

13

The koala lives in the eucalyptus forests of eastern Australia.

If the koala is to survive, its habitat must be protected.

A koala...

clings to its mother's back.

has only a stub of a tail.

has thick, woolly fur.

sees during the day or night.

identifies leaves through its sense of smell before eating them.

uses two thumbs and three fingers to grip branches.

Glossary/Index